W9-CBV-014

The HUMANE SOCIETIES

A · VOICE · FOR · THE · ANIMALS

Shelley Swanson Sateren

Dillon Press · Parsippany, New Jersey

To my dear mom and dad, who let me have every kind of pet I ever wanted, except a skunk.—S.S.S

Acknowledgments

Many thanks to Betsy Tyus of the American Humane Association for her tremendous help in providing information for this book and for her expert reading of the manuscript. Special thanks also to Wendy Kerich for the book idea and to Judy Dworkin of the Animal Humane Society of Hennepin County, Minneapolis, for providing much information and support. I am also grateful to the following agencies and individuals for their help with this book: the American Humane Association [AHA]; the American Society for the Prevention of Cruelty to Animals [ASPCA]; the Humane Society of the United States [HSUS]; the World Society for the Protection of Animals [WSPA]; Wim deKok of the WSPA; Janelle Fowlds of the Becker County Humane Society; Michael Kaufmann of the AHA; Priscilla McMullen of the WSPA; Ron Sadowsky; Roald Sateren; Keith Streff, Abuse Investigator for the Animal Humane Society of Hennepin County; Celia Waldock of the Humane Society of Ramsey County.

Library of Congress Cataloging-in-Publication Data

Sateren, Shelley Swanson.
 The humane societies: a voice for the animals/by Shelley Swanson Sateren.—1st ed.
 p. cm.
 Includes index.
 Summary: Explains how members of humane societies use methods such as adoption to deal with problems including animal overpopulation and abandonment.
 ISBN 0-87518-622-X (lib. bdg.). ISBN 0-382-39309-0 (pbk.)
 1. Animal welfare—United States—Societies, etc.—Juvenile literature. [1. Animals—Treatment.] I. Title.
 HV4763.S37 1997
 179'.3'0973—dc20   95-35445

Photo Credits

Front Cover: Norvia Behling
Back Cover: Ronald Levy
American Humane Association, Colorado: 7, 68. Animal Humane Society of Hennepin County, Minneapolis: 28, 34, 57, 60, 64. ASPCA, New York: 15. Norvia Behling: 4, 6, 11, 22, 32, 37, 39, 42, 45, 48, 50. Richard Gibbons: 20. Kurt Grebner: 21. Humane Society of Ramsey County, St. Paul: 27. Ronald Levy: 12. Milwaukee Sentinel: 71. WSPA, Boston: 73.

Cover and book design by Lisa Ann Arcuri

Published by Dillon Press
A Division of Simon & Schuster
299 Jefferson Road, Parsippany, NJ 07054

First Edition
Printed in the United States of America
10 9 8 7 6 5 4 3 2 1

Contents

Max, a Dalmatian, is waiting to be adopted.

Max, Lucy, and Sanuk: Three of the 13 Million

"Heel Max," commands a volunteer dog walker. "Good boy!" The volunteer leads Max, a Dalmatian, out of the animal shelter's front door for Max's morning walk.

Inside the adoption center, another volunteer cuddles a guinea pig after cleaning its cage. "You're sweet, yes you are," the volunteer coos in the guinea pig's ear.

At the information desk the receptionist answers the phone and listens for a minute to the caller's concern. "If you think your neighbor's dog has been locked in the garage for that long," the receptionist tells the caller, "then you'd better report it to Larry, our abuse investigator. Hold on, please, I'll connect you."

A father and son look for a kitten at a shelter.

It's Saturday morning at the city humane society, the busiest day of the week at the animal shelter. Dozens of people stream through the reception area to the two rooms containing cat and kitten cages, and then down the long hallway to the dog kennels. Barking echoes through the shelter corridors as the canines greet their many human visitors.

The dogs wag their tails and yip expectantly at the people parading past the kennels. "Please adopt me!" the canines seem to say. And that's exactly why these people are here—they're looking for pets to adopt.

Downstairs from the adoption center is the receiving room. People enter through the side door off the lower parking lot, carrying cats in blankets or kittens in cardboard boxes or trailing dogs on leashes.

Beside the receiving counter, a young girl wipes her eyes unhappily. Quietly the girl and her mother say good-bye to their tabby cat. They have to give the animal away because the girl has developed allergies.

This tabby is the fourth cat surrendered to the shelter in the half-hour since the doors opened this morning. There are already 87 animals in the shelter today, and more will likely arrive throughout the afternoon.

These animals all have two things in common—they are homeless and they are

These dogs seem to call out from their kennel, "Please adopt me!"

waiting. Many wait to be adopted. Others wait for their veterinary examinations that will help determine whether they're adoptable. Still others are strays that recently arrived at the shelter. They wait to be found by and reunited with their owners.

Lucy

Minutes after the tabby cat arrives at the shelter, a man enters the receiving door, tugging a panting, overweight English bulldog by its leash. The man yanks on the leash, trying to keep the bulldog at his side while he reads the sign above the receiving counter. The sign says:

ANIMALS SURRENDERED TO US BECOME THE PROPERTY OF THIS HUMANE SOCIETY. OUR HOLDING FACILITIES ARE LIMITED AND OFTEN OVERCROWDED. WE WILL DECIDE WITHIN 24 HOURS IF AN ANIMAL WILL BE PUT UP FOR ADOPTION; ANIMALS NOT PUT UP FOR ADOPTION WILL BE PUT TO SLEEP WITH A LETHAL INJECTION.

"Wouldn't you know," the man tells the staff worker behind the counter, "my daughter got married, and my wife and I got stuck with her dog. My wife just had new carpet put in, and she can't stand the dog anyhow. I hate to give the dog away, but I don't have any choice."

The man signs the necessary papers, pays the surrender donation, then leaves Lucy behind. Suddenly, Lucy is homeless. What becomes of her will depend in part on her age, her health, and her temperament.

A staff worker leads Lucy back to the kennels. The worker gives her food and water and several pats on her head. Lucy sits down and looks around her, appearing perplexed. Now she'll have to wait her turn—about an hour—for her veterinary exam.

Sanuk

Soon after Lucy's ex-owner leaves the shelter, a woman enters the receiving door. "We moved to a new apartment, and our cat got out," the woman tells the staff employee. "He's been missing for a week. Could I check Lost and Found again today?"

"Of course," replies the employee. He leads the woman down the hall to a small room where the found adult cats are boarding. In a far cage on the top row lies a Siamese cat, silently licking its paw.

The woman stands on tiptoe and peers in the cage. "That's him!" she cries. "Oh Sanuk, you're here. Oh, I can't believe it!"

"It's terrific when people find their animals," the employee tells the woman and smiles. "Someone brought your cat in just yesterday."

"I'm so glad!" The woman signs the required papers and then leaves the shelter, holding Sanuk tightly in her arms.

Max

Back upstairs in the adoption center, a family considers adopting Max, the Dalmatian. The family takes Max for a walk and then plays with him for a while in the shelter courtyard. Spending time alone with Max helps the family make this important decision.

"Can we adopt him, Dad?" the boy asks. "He's a great dog!"

"I think he's the dog for us," agrees the boy's father.

The boy fills out the adoption application, and his father signs the contract. Max now has a new home. After several weeks of being homeless, his waiting days are over.

A stray, Max had been found and turned into the city dog shelter. He was held there for the allowed stay of seven days, then was turned over to the humane society for possible adoption. The shelter held Max for four days to check his health and temperament—which were both fine. Then he was placed in a foster home for a week.

Max is united with an owner who will give him a new, loving home.

It was the foster family's job to decide whether this stray would make a good pet. After spending a week with Max, the family decided he'd make a terrific companion animal. The foster family returned him to the shelter, where he spent a week and a half on the adoption floor.

Today is Max's lucky Saturday. The boy scans the shelves of pet supplies for sale in the adoption center and buys a rubber ball for Max. The boy gives Max his toy and a big hug. Then the family takes Max to his new home. If he's fortunate, it will also be his final home.

Max, Lucy, and Sanuk are just three of the millions of abandoned, runaway, or surrendered animals that arrive at humane society

Dogs and horses are two of the many kinds of animals given shelter at humane societies.

shelters each year. Every year, shelters receive more than 13 million animals that have nowhere else to go. Humane societies have sheltered all kinds of animals, including pigs, cows, ponies, raccoons, beavers, dogs, cats, rabbits, birds, and rodents—even lions and tigers.

For wild animals that are wounded, the goal of humane societies is to rehabilitate the animals and release them into the wild, if possible. Or they may be placed with a licensed rehabilitator or nature center. For domesticated animals, such as dogs and cats, the goal is to place as many as possible into new homes. This is a good thing for Max and for thousands of other animals that are happily adopted from humane societies each year.

Humane Societies Then and Today

One hundred fifty years ago in the United States, the idea that people should be kind to animals was new and unusual. America was a young nation, much of it still frontier. In this rapidly growing, rough young country, animals were valued mainly for the amount of work they could accomplish.

A Hard Life

Kindness to animals wasn't a consideration in the mid-1800s. Most Americans believed that animals were put on Earth for people to use and even abuse, if necessary. For example, cruelty to horses was commonplace. Central to work forces, these hard-working animals toiled steadily without food or rest—even in the worst weather conditions. They were beaten if they slowed their pace.

In those days before the automobile, horses were also the primary means of transportation. Many carriage and cart horses were abused by their drivers every day, in American cities.

Dogs too had little worth. The main purpose of urban animal control agencies was to clear their cities of stray dogs. To get rid of strays, policemen shot them in the streets. Poundmasters also drowned dogs, in full view of the public's curious eye.

In New York City in the 1850s and 1860s, as many as 300 dogs were caught every day and drowned, while crowds of people looked on and cheered. Dog drownings were common in other cities, including Minneapolis, where strays were placed in cages and then lowered into the Mississippi River. Hundreds of children frequently watched the spectacle from the waterfront.

Eventually, across the country, concerned citizens began to object to these inhumane practices. One man, Henry Bergh, was especially disturbed by the cruel treatment of underfed and overworked draft horses. In 1866 he established an animal protection agency in New York City—the first humane organization in the United States. This was the American Society for the Prevention of Cruelty to Animals. Thanks to the work of Henry Bergh and his new organization, the New York State legislature passed the first law in America

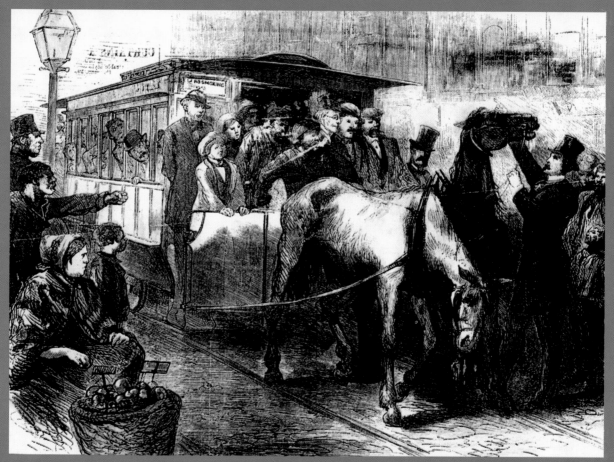

Henry Bergh came to the rescue of overworked horses. He established the first humane organization in the United States. Bergh is shown in this lithograph holding the horse's reins.

making cruelty to animals a crime.

Before long, people founded humane societies in other cities, all with the goal of working to protect animals. Some were established to safeguard children as well as animals. The societies took different names, such as Anticruelty Society or Animal Rescue League or Dumb Friends' League. They all believed, as Henry Bergh did, that people should help protect animals from needless suffering.

United in Kindness

In the United States today, about 3,000 humane societies exist across the country. When a group of people sets up an animal welfare organization, the founding members are free to choose any name they want for it, such as Maplewood Society for the Protection of Animals or Humane Society of Apple County or Noah's Ark League. Humane societies also range in size—anywhere from eight cages in a small mountain town to a capacity of 600 animals or more in a city shelter.

The several thousand American humane societies are independent of each other in finances and operations, but they share common beliefs about animal welfare. Their philosophy is simple: People should treat all animals as kindly as possible. If people can't or won't treat animals kindly, humane societies feel it's their duty to look after the suffering or homeless animals.

Humane societies also share common goals. They work to educate the public in how to care properly for domestic animals. They also educate people about how to be responsible and committed adopters of pets. And they work to protect both domestic and wild animals from cruelty and neglect.

Animal Welfare, Animal Rights

The basic goals and beliefs of humane societies are concerned with "animal welfare" instead of "animal rights." Humane societies differ from animal rights groups in a number of ways.

Animal rights groups believe that animals have the right not to be killed, eaten, or used for sport or research. Some animal rights groups disagree with the philosophies of humane societies, saying the societies compromise in these areas.

Humane societies don't all call for a total ban on animals used in research, sports, and entertainment. But they do protest activities in these areas that cause animals unnecessary pain and suffering. Two examples are the cruel sports of dogfighting and cockfighting.

Humane societies may share certain objectives with some animal rights groups, but they differ in their methods of bringing about change. Some animal rights groups use boycotts, pickets, and at times even illegal means to rescue suffering animals or animals likely to be killed. Humane societies work within the limits of the law to make social and legislative changes regarding the treatment of animals.

Who Controls the Strays?

The goals of humane societies also differ from animal control agencies. Animal control agencies were once commonly known as dog pounds. They are responsible for licensing and controlling animals that run loose on the streets or that create a nuisance in neighborhoods. They also enforce the laws regarding animals. There are some animal control agencies that are strictly holding centers for strays. They board the animals for a maximum number of days—usually about a week. Then, if the animals aren't claimed by their owners, they are euthanized—painlessly put to death.

However, in the past ten to fifteen years, many animal control agencies have started programs that are similar to those of humane societies. Most now put pets up for adoption. Others pass strays on to humane societies, which in turn put the animals on the adoption floor.

In some areas, animal control agencies and humane societies are required by law to release unclaimed shelter animals to research facilities instead of euthanizing them. These animals must be given to university laboratories, research facilities, or cosmetic and drug manufacturers. The scientists and manufacturers use the animals as test subjects for everything from new cancer drugs to new household cleaners. These animals often suffer pain and trauma from the tests performed on them.

Humane societies and animal control agencies located in these areas are fighting to get the laws changed. Shelters exist to provide animals with safe havens until they are adopted, returned to their owners, or humanely killed. If an owner knows that a pet may be released to a research facility, he or she may be less likely to turn the animal in to a shelter and may abandon it instead. Public trust and confidence in the shelter is then destroyed.

Dog Dashes and Phone-a-thons

State laws affect animal control agencies and humane societies in another important way. Local governments across the United States keep animal control agencies operating with the support of tax dollars. This is not true of humane society shelters. Humane societies are nonprofit organizations, unlike breeders and pet shops, and they receive no government funding. They depend entirely on fund-raisers and donations from the public— donations of money, equipment, or dog food—to keep their shelters operating.

Popular fund-raisers at shelters include

Dogs and their owners help raise money for shelters in K9-5K runs.

raffles, craft and bake sales, and phone-a-thons. Shelters also have sports events to raise money. People collect pledges and then walk or run in Dog Dashes or K9–5K runs with their dogs. Spending a Saturday afternoon running a race with the family pet is lots of fun for both the human and canine participants.

All across America, volunteers share their time and talents to raise money for humane societies. Contributions may be small, such as making cookies for a bake sale, or contributions may be very generous, such as those that a volunteer named Ron Sadowsky has offered.

In 1990, Ron took pledges and ran 152 miles through Death Valley, Nevada.

During the time he ran, the temperature was 120 degrees Fahrenheit, with the ground temperature at 200 degrees Fahrenheit. As he ran, heat from the ground came through his shoes and burned his feet. In breaks during the run, Ron's body was wrapped in ice to bring his temperature back down. By running through Death Valley, Ron raised $21,000 for his local humane society shelter in Minnesota. This generous volunteer ran the same course again in 1993 and earned $17,000 for his local shelter.

There are ways that children too may get involved in humane society volunteer work. Helping shelters with fund-raisers is one way. Many children enjoy selling

Ron Sadowsky runs in Death Valley to raise funds for needy animals.

raffle tickets, collecting pledges, working at booths, and walking or running in Dog Dashes with their pets.

People Who Care About Animals

Humane societies also rely on volunteers to help operate the shelters. Most of the societies have few paid employees because money is scarce. So shelters must depend on assistance from volunteers to help all the needy animals.

Volunteers give their time, talents, and love in many ways. They groom the animals, serve as office assistants, walk dogs, work at special events, and clean cages. Some shelters have Youth Volunteer programs where volunteer teenagers

A teenage volunteer helps groom a shelter dog.

exercise and groom dogs and help with customer service and adoption.

As with all nonprofit organizations, volunteers are crucial to maintaining operations at humane societies. The shelters also depend on their committed employees, who are willing to work for low pay. Wendy, a part-time employee at a shelter in Minnesota, makes $5.15 an hour.

"I have two years of veterinary-technician education, so I could do research at the university," says Wendy. "But I love working here at the shelter in spite of the low pay. I feel like I'm doing a good thing."

Anne, a full-time employee at the same shelter, recalls, "I wanted to work here ever since sixth grade, after I toured the shelter on a school field trip." Years later, as an adult, Anne began volunteer work at the shelter and was soon hired to be on the staff. She doesn't complain about the low pay because, she insists, "I love the work so much!"

Whether they are volunteers or paid employees, people who work at local shelters across America are people who care about animals. Committed humane society volunteers and employees also work at the national and international levels. There are two main national humane societies in America—the American Humane Association (AHA) and the Humane Society of the United

States (HSUS). There is one main international humane society—the World Society for the Protection of Animals (WSPA). The national agencies are involved in all areas of animal welfare and protection in North America, and WSPA helps animals throughout the world.

Local humane society shelters are independent of the AHA, HSUS, and WSPA. But they all share common beliefs and similar stands on animal welfare policies.

The HSUS, AHA, and WSPA are sizable agencies that are able to tackle larger animal protection issues. Smaller local societies are sometimes limited in what they can do. Local shelters are concerned about the welfare of all animals, but their immediate concern is for the needy animals in their area. This might be a box of kittens abandoned in a ditch, a retired tiger from a zoo, or a truckload of cattle that's stranded on a freeway. The doors of humane society shelters are open to all animals in need.

Shelter From the Storm

Why must America have 3,000 humane society shelters? And why must more than 13 million animals pass through these shelters' doors each year? Who is responsible for this staggering problem?

Pet owners are the primary responsible party. The number one reason that companion animals end up at shelters is because they've become inconvenient or impossible to keep, so their owners give them up or abandon them.

Good-bye, Rex

People give their companion animals away to shelters for many different reasons. Some people must give their pets away during hard economic times because they can no longer afford to feed the animals or provide proper veterinary care.

This was common during the Great Depression of the 1930s and the recession of the late 1980s and early 1990s.

Pets are also surrendered when adults start new jobs with difficult work schedules—leaving too little time to care for their animals. And often people are forced to give up their animals when they move to rental housing that doesn't allow pets. Some of the saddest surrenders occur when elderly people move to retirement homes that won't allow pets. This situation forces many to give away their beloved companion animals.

Other owners turn their pets in to shelters not because circumstances force them to but because they just don't feel like being pet owners anymore. They discard their pets merely because they're tired of them, like the woman from Pennsylvania who gave her older dog away to a shelter because he wouldn't play anymore. The dog had become tired in his old age, and his owner grew bored with him.

A Lifetime Commitment

Some owners surrender their companion animals because they don't understand the importance of being committed to a pet for a lifetime—the lifetime of the animal, that is. With good care most cats and dogs can live to be 10 to 15 years old or even older. Before people buy or adopt a

A homeless cat sits in its shelter cage after being surrendered by its owners who moved out of state.

pet, they need to anticipate changes that could occur in their household during the animal's life span. Might the family move away to a new town or city? Will a new baby join the household? Changes such as these could affect the lifetime commitment to a pet.

Dogs and cats become very attached to their homes and human families, and it's traumatic for them to be given away. Companion animals need permanent, caring homes.

A lack of lifelong commitment to a pet is often the result of impulse buying. This occurs frequently at shopping malls throughout America. Many people strolling through the malls are unable to

Owners and their pets often become very attached to each other.

resist the adorable young animals for sale in pet shop windows. People often go to a mall with no intention of looking for a pet but wind up buying an irresistible puppy or kitten on a whim.

Soon after taking the puppy or kitten home, reality sets in. Impulse pet buyers discover that feeding a companion animal and paying for its veterinary visits can be costly. Or they learn that it requires work, time, and patience to tend to an animal's needs and to train it properly. Or the pet grows up and doesn't look cute anymore. The novelty wears off and the pet is given away to a shelter. This is a big problem at humane society shelters across the country. There are too many "teenage" animals that were given away because they were no longer adorably tiny or small enough to manage.

A lack of commitment also often occurs when people receive "free pets." Free pets are animals that are given to others at no cost by friends, neighbors, or relatives. Or the pets are received as gifts or found through advertisements in newspapers. The problem is that when something is obtained for nothing, people often place little or no value on it. It's easy for them to discard something that they consider to be worthless. Unfortunately, very few free pets find permanent, loving homes. Approximately two-thirds of them end up in animal shelters.

Problem Pets

Sometimes companion animals are surrendered because their owners consider them to be problem pets that can't be trained or controlled. When discipline and "acting out" problems arise with pets, proper training can often combat these problems. But it takes time and effort on the part of the pet owner to find out what the training techniques are and how to put them into practice. When owners can't or won't do this, many of these animals wind up in shelters.

Sometimes animals are labeled problem pets because of a language barrier between the owners and their animals.

At times, pets communicate through scratching or biting, by having urinating accidents, or by barking too much or too loudly. When they do these things, they are trying to tell their owners something. They are often saying that they are lonely, bored, jealous, sick, or perhaps frightened.

For instance, a normally quiet, well-behaved cat was turned in to a shelter in Colorado because she had recently begun to cry a lot. The cat's owner couldn't stand her constant crying and gave her away. Not long before, the cat had lost her companion—another cat, which had died—and she was crying out of loneliness. Her owner didn't understand this, and he dealt with the noise problem by surrendering the cat to a shelter.

Sometimes a pet's behavior problem can be corrected if the owner changes his or her own behavior. For example, not leaving a lonely dog at home by itself for too long can help stop problem barking. Or teaching a toddler to treat a cat gently can help prevent the cat from scratching the child.

It's important for children of all ages to learn to treat animals with respect. This is one way of avoiding problem behavior in pets. It's important too that parents teach their babies and toddlers not to squeeze animals tightly or pull their hair. Even the most gentle animal can be frightened or startled by a child treating it roughly, and it may hurt the child in self-defense.

Of all children, eight- to ten-year-old boys are most often bitten by dogs, because they tease the animals, run from them, or scream. These boys and all children need to learn not to wrestle with dogs and never to pet an unfamiliar dog or look it directly in the eye. If children learn to treat animals gently and with respect, fewer cases of biting and scratching will occur. Then fewer problem animals will be given away to shelters.

Abandoned Animals

Some pet owners don't give their unwanted pets away to shelters but abandon

Children can learn to respect animals and to treat them with kindness.

them instead. When these people get tired of their pets or can't keep them anymore, they desert the animals or let them go or lock them out of the house. Every year in May, college students leave cats behind in empty dorm rooms. Every month of the year, renters move away and leave pets behind in empty apartments. Throughout the year, all across America, puppies and kittens are abandoned in ditches or dropped into dumpsters.

Why do some pet owners abandon their animals instead of taking them to humane society shelters? Some people fear the animals will be euthanized. Others can't stand the thought of their pets being in cages. These people believe that their unwanted pets are better off abandoned than in a humane society shelter.

The truth is that an abandoned animal has less than a two-year life expectancy living on its own. An owner shows greater concern for a pet by giving it to a shelter than by turning the animal loose to manage by itself on a city street or in the country. On its own the animal will likely starve, freeze, become sick, be attacked by other animals, or get hit by a car. It will surely die a premature death. But if the animal were given to a humane society shelter, it would have medical care, food, exercise, a warm and safe kennel to sleep in, and a chance to be adopted.

Abandoned kittens such as these are likely to die a premature death.

Some people abandon their unwanted pets instead of taking them to shelters to avoid paying a surrender fee. But a surrender fee is rarely required at humane society shelters. Most just ask for a donation, and some don't ask for one at all.

Sometimes people find abandoned dogs and cats and decide not to take the strays to shelters. Instead, they decide to care for the animals themselves. In the long run this often hurts the animals rather than helps them. Many new caretakers learn that providing food and veterinary fees for the animals is too expensive. Or they discover they don't have enough time to devote to the animals. Or they already have too many pets to care for.

Often the stray dogs and cats are abandoned again. If a person finds a stray, the humane response is to take the animal to a shelter.

Abandoning an animal is not only inhumane, it's against the law. People act legally and responsibly when they take their unwanted pets to humane society shelters. Everyone benefits when pet owners do this. The animals are better off than they would be if they were abandoned. And the American public also benefits, because it costs taxpayers $800 million every year to control these homeless animals.

On the walls of receiving centers in many shelters hang signs that say the following:

**THANK YOU
FOR BRINGING YOUR
PET TO THIS
HUMANE SOCIETY,
INSTEAD OF TURNING
IT LOOSE.**

Perhaps if dogs and cats could talk, they too would thank the people who brought them to the shelters. Thousands of those once-unwanted animals now have an excellent chance of being adopted. Happily, many will find permanent, loving homes.

Chapter 4

New Homes for the Homeless

One weekend in a small Wisconsin town, a girl and her mother decide it's finally time to find a furry new addition to their family. They've wanted a cat for a long time.

They drive to the county humane society shelter in a nearby town, and the girl looks over all the cats. A three-year-old male tiger cat named Tigger catches her eye. Then Tigger licks the girl's hand, and he captures her heart.

"He's the one I want!" the girl tells her mother excitedly.

A Helpful Counselor

Before they adopt Tigger, the girl and her mother spend about 15 minutes in a counseling session with a shelter employee. The counselor asks them several questions: Who in the family will be responsible for Tigger's care? Do they understand the financial commitment involved in owning a pet? Do they have any concerns about giving Tigger the lifetime care that he needs? The girl and her mother answer the counselor's questions and then ask several of their own about how to care for Tigger properly.

Preadoption counseling sessions such as this one are becoming increasingly common at humane society shelters across America. Many shelters now require them. Humane societies want to make sure that shelter animals are going to

Tigger is adopted by a loving and caring owner.

responsible adoptive families. Part of being a responsible pet owner, counselors point out to adopters, is following local laws for immunization and licensing, taking pets to veterinarians for regular physicals, and having dogs and cats wear identification tags at all times.

Counselors also try to find out if new adopters will be committed to the companion animals for the life span of the pets. The animals have already been given away and put up for adoption once. Humane societies don't want the animals to have to go through this experience twice.

In talking with adopters, counselors sometimes discover that people are adopting animals out of sympathy. Some people who visit shelters are troubled when they see all of the animals in cages. They find themselves thinking about those that may die and those that may live, and they wish they could take all of them home. But it's important that people adopt pets because they want them, not because they feel sorry for them. Sympathy is not a solid foundation for a lasting relationship. Counselors know from experience that "sympathy adoptions" are not committed adoptions and that the animals will most likely be brought back to the shelters. When counselors suspect a sympathy adoption, they usually don't approve it.

Preadoption counseling also helps shelter employees find out if a certain type of pet is appropriate for an adopter. Suppose a family wants to adopt a dog, but both parents work full-time and the children are involved in after-school music and sports programs. A shelter counselor will likely suggest to a family this busy that they adopt a low-maintenance pet, such as a gerbil or a bird or a guinea pig, instead of a dog. These pets require less time and attention than canines.

To help avoid mismatches with families, counselors will also make recommendations about adopting a pet of a certain age. Families with small children, for instance, frequently want to adopt puppies, but

Pets such as gerbils are low maintenance pets.

counselors know that housebreaking puppies can be difficult. It often proves too much for parents to handle when they're also very busy caring for babies and toddlers. Counselors sometimes suggest that these families adopt older dogs that are already housebroken.

Counselors will make suggestions such as these at times, but they rarely turn down a person or family altogether. A counselor won't approve an adoption if the person lives in an apartment but doesn't have the landlord's permission to keep a pet. Or a counselor will say "no" if a person already has more pets than local law allows, since some counties prohibit having too many pets in a household. Or a family will be turned down if it's clear to the counselor that the children want the animal but the parents don't care much for the idea of owning a pet. Counselors know that mothers and fathers usually take on most of the responsibility for pet care, so it's important that parents feel ready for a lifetime commitment to the animals.

Preadoption counseling exists to make sure that animals go to committed and appropriate homes. Discussing possible problems helps avoid adoptions that "just didn't work out." Having to take an animal back to a shelter is a very unpleasant experience for the family as well as for the animal. Humane societies want to help avoid that. Counseling programs at shelters help create happier adoptive families and happier and healthier pets. And this means fewer animals returned to shelters.

Back at the shelter in Wisconsin, the girl and her mother who want to adopt the cat named Tigger finish their counseling session. The counselor approves the adoption and the girl and her mother leave with their new cat. Tigger, once-unwanted, now has a loving new home.

A Healthy Pet for a Fine Price

Giving a homeless animal a new home is just one reason that many people choose to adopt a pet rather than buy one. Adopting pets from humane society shelters—instead of buying them from breeders or pet shops—also saves people money. A person may pay $200 to $500 for an animal at a pet shop or from a breeder, while the average cost of adopting a dog or cat from a humane society shelter is $40 to $60.

Shelter adoption fees usually include an animal's first set of vaccinations and a veterinary exam. In many cases the medical services a pet has already received at a shelter are equal in value to—and are sometimes more than—the entire adoption fee. Adoption costs don't begin to cover shelter expenses. The goal of humane societies is to take care of homeless animals, not to make a profit on them.

All shelter animals are given exams by trained veterinarians.

Since animals receive shots and a physical at humane society shelters, adopters can usually count on getting a healthy pet. Many shelters have a healthy-pet guarantee for a period of time—usually about a week—following the day of the pet's adoption. If the adopted animal turns out to be unhealthy during that time, it may be returned to the shelter. The adopters may get their money back or pick out a different animal.

Puppy Mills

Unlike these shelters, which make every attempt to place healthy animals, many pet stores can't make the same promise. Some pet shops are more concerned with making a profit than with ensuring the health of their animals. People can't be guaranteed that they will always receive healthy animals from some pet shops because very often the stores get their puppies from "puppy mills." Puppy mills are breeding farms that supply pet-store animals. Puppy mills produce as many dogs as possible for the lowest price. The breeders save money by not providing proper care and housing for the animals. Raised in neglect, animals from puppy mills are at great risk for disturbed personalities and poor health.

Many animals raised at puppy mills suffer in cruel conditions. Confined to small, dirty cages, they have little protection in poor weather, aren't fed well, and are sometimes abused. Some of them die in their cages. Those that live have little or no positive contact with humans. Descendants of wolves, dogs are still, after thousands of years of domestication, social animals. They need to be cuddled and played with, especially when they're puppies. Animals raised in puppy mills don't receive this necessary affection and attention from humans, so they don't grow up to be good house pets. They are nervous, likely to bite people, and sometimes unable to be housebroken.

Female dogs at puppy mills give birth to litter after litter, with little time to regain their strength in between. Their puppies are taken away from them at the very early age of seven weeks, packed into trucks, and driven for miles to pet stores. Many of the puppies don't survive the journey because of their young age and poor health. Either they catch diseases or the truck ride is more than they can handle.

When people choose to adopt dogs rather than buy them, they help put puppy mills out of business. Less demand for puppies at pet stores means fewer litters will be born and raised at these breeding farms.

All Sorts of Best Friends

Besides being guaranteed a healthy pet, many people adopt animals from humane society shelters because they're able to find the kind of pet they want there. Both purebred and mixed-breed animals are available for adoption at humane societies.

Often, people prefer to own mixed-breed dogs, and at shelters there are all sorts to choose from. Many people believe that mixed-breed dogs make great pets because they tend to have friendlier personalities and better health than some purebred animals. Many dog owners believe that mixed breeds, or mutts, are the best choice of all because they have a totally unique appearance and may also combine some of the best traits of their different breed ancestors.

Sometimes, though, people want a particular breed of dog or cat but can't find that

Mixed-breed dogs, such as this shepherd-mix puppy, are often good choices for adoption.

certain animal at their local shelter. If they choose to go to a breeder, they would be wise to find a breeder with a good reputation to be assured of getting a happy, healthy animal.

Many people choose to adopt animals from shelters—instead of buying them from stores or breeders—to save money and to save animals' lives. There are thousands of "best friends" just waiting to be adopted at shelters across America. People can find wonderful, lifelong companions there. By adopting pets from humane societies, people are helping to save lives—because there simply aren't enough homes for all of the animals.

No Room in the Ark

In a city humane society shelter, a small poodle-mix dog huddles in his cage. "I suspect he was abused by his owner," says a staff worker as she fills the dog's water dish. "He's so shy and nervous."

After two weeks on the adoption floor, the frightened dog remains unwanted. He's just too afraid of people. At the end of the second week, a shelter employee takes him off the adoption floor and leads him away. Unadoptable animals have to be removed to make space for incoming animals, who arrive hourly in the receiving center.

One of the new arrivals is a five-year-old male border collie. "I'm moving to an apartment and I can't keep him anymore," the owner explains to the shelter employee. But unfortunately for this older dog, the shelter has many puppies that are also up for adoption this week.

More Americans prefer to adopt puppies rather than adult dogs, and this is also true of kittens and cats. Dogs and cats alike become adult at about one year of age. Puppies and kittens are very popular with adopters, and the older animals are often left behind in shelters.

The majority of these adult animals are perfectly fine, obedient, and friendly. But many people won't consider adopting adult dogs or cats, especially if the animals are older than five or six years of age.

The five-year-old border collie in the city shelter is one that's overlooked because of his age. He and the frightened poodle-mix dog in the same shelter both meet a similar end. They are humanely put to death.

A Pet-Overpopulation Crisis

Every year in the United States, 22 million dogs and cats are born. More than 13 million are turned in to shelters. And of these, about 7 million are euthanized. The number euthanized each year is more than the human populations of Wisconsin, Minnesota, and North and South Dakota combined.

Some of the animals are euthanized because their temperament, older age, or poor health makes them unadoptable. But most die because there aren't enough homes for all of the homeless animals.

Shelter workers across the country wish they could keep all of the incoming animals until they're adopted. But this just isn't always possible. Either there's not enough money—it costs about nine dollars a day for a humane society to keep one animal—or there isn't enough room, since more homeless animals arrive daily.

A pet-overpopulation crisis exists in America today. Many people bring their older unwanted pets or their litters of kittens and puppies to humane societies, believing the shelters can find a new owner for every animal. This isn't true.

Pet overpopulation is a big problem for shelters, with unwanted litters arriving daily.

There are millions more companion animals than there are homes to care for them. Shelters are overcrowded with adult companion animals because owners weren't committed to their pets. And shelters are crowded with kittens and puppies because owners allow their pets to have babies. Every year in America, seven times more puppies and kittens are born than human babies.

Some pet owners allow their dogs or cats to have litters, claiming they'll find homes for all the babies. But the owners are not always able to place the entire litter. And even if they do, this takes available homes away from the thousands of animals already waiting in line to be adopted.

Spaying and Neutering

Sometimes people allow their pets to have litters because they want the children in the family to learn about the miracle of birth. But birthrates this high—22 million dogs and cats born every year—are major problems, not miracles. What's miraculous is that some of these animals find loving, lifetime homes.

Other pets are permitted to breed when their owners allow them to roam the neighborhood even though the animals haven't been spayed or neutered. Spaying and neutering are operations performed by a veterinarian in which an animal's reproductive organs are removed. This prevents the animal from becoming a parent. Spaying is the operation that alters a female animal. The term *neuter* generally refers to the operation that alters a male.

Some people don't have their pets spayed or neutered because they can't pay the veterinary fee. But many humane society shelters in America have assistance programs that help people afford the cost of spaying and neutering. Often owners are entitled to the programs even if they haven't adopted pets from these shelters.

Many pet owners don't have their dogs spayed or neutered because they believe the operation will have an unfavorable effect on their canines. Some believe a spayed female dog will become lazy and

Pets that have been neutered or spayed often become better tempered.

overweight. Others believe a neutered male dog won't hunt or be as protective or playful. But spaying a female won't cause her to gain weight—too much food and too little exercise will. And an altered male will continue to guard his owner's home, will remain just as lively and playful, and will still be able to act as a hunting dog.

Spaying and neutering benefit companion animals in many ways—and they benefit the animals' owners, too. These pets are often more mild-mannered and affectionate, and they also have decreased chances of getting certain types of diseases and infections.

When people don't spay or neuter their pets and allow them to mate, the effect on pet overpopulation can be enormous. An unspayed dog and her unspayed descendants can produce as many as 4,000 dogs in only seven years, if they're all allowed to breed.

Just one unspayed cat and her unspayed litter can contribute even more animals to the population explosion, if permitted to breed. Consider the mathematical results: A female cat mates and in just three months her kittens are born. She could have a litter of as many as six kittens, three of which might be female. Soon, if allowed to mate, the females would have litters of their own, about six babies each. In a few months more there would be about eighty cats. If their kittens were also allowed to breed, in one year the feline family could consist of about 250 cats. If this one family of unaltered felines continued to breed unchecked, as many as 150,000 cats could come into the world in just seven years.

Shelters across America receive thousands of kittens in need of homes every year between spring and autumn—the cat-breeding season. The problem is that unwanted adult cats continue to be brought into shelters during this time, too. But the adult cats rarely get adopted during "kitten season," because adopters are drawn to the babies. As a result, more adult cats are euthanized during kitten season.

Pet owners act humanely and responsibly when they spay or neuter their companion animals. Owners should check with their veterinarians to find out the best age to spay or neuter their pets. Generally, females should be spayed at about six months of age, and males should be neutered at about nine months. If owners wait longer, unwanted litters may follow.

Humane societies believe that prevention is the key to solving the problem of pet-overpopulation. Shelter veterinarians spay or neuter many animals before they're put up for adoption. If puppies or kittens are still too young for the operation, their adopters sign a contract agreeing to have the animals spayed or neutered within 30 days after the animals reach adulthood. Most shelters have a follow-up system to make sure the adopters spay or neuter their pets.

A Humane Death

In spite of these efforts, the overpopulation crisis remains, and shelters continue to work hard to increase adoption rates. Some humane societies send their animals to different shelters, hoping they'll have better luck finding homes there. Others have "adoption fairs" at town squares or shopping areas to bring the animals into contact with more adopters. Occasionally shelters are able to hold ani-

mals for a long time—some are held for as long as three to five months—to increase the animals' chances of getting adopted.

But because money and space are in short supply, most shelters are forced to have holding-period limits. The average holding period at shelters in America is two weeks.

When serious efforts to find caring and responsible homes for all of the adoptable animals fail, some of the animals must be humanely put to death. Humane societies believe that euthanasia is the kindest means of dealing with unwanted animals. Their philosophy is to take the action that will eventually, if not immediately, do the most to protect animals from pain, fear, and suffering.

Today the majority of shelters use the most humane means known for euthanizing animals—an injection of sodium pentobarbital. Death by this injection is almost instantaneous. It is also completely painless if the task is performed correctly. Well-attended workshops that teach employees how to give animals pain-free injections are held at shelters across the country. Still, euthanasia is a bleak task for every humane society employee who performs it.

Some people in America don't believe in euthanasia. They protest it, saying, "Surely there must be a better way." Those who feel strongly about the issue sometimes set up "no-kill" shelters to avoid euthanizing homeless companion animals. No-kill animal shelters do save lives, but only those of a small number of the homeless, needy animals in America. Most no-kill shelters screen incoming animals and take only adoptable pets, such as healthy kittens and puppies. If animals are sick or older than five years of age, most no-kill shelters will not take them. The needier animals wind up at humane society shelters or at animal control agencies.

There is a way, however, to lessen the problem. If everyone spayed or neutered his or her pet, animal shelters would not have to euthanize millions of unwanted cats and dogs every year.

People also help when they discourage their friends from breeding their pets, when they adopt homeless animals from humane societies, and when they choose to adopt adult dogs or cats for companions. These actions can help save many animals from needless suffering.

6

Round-the-Clock Compassion

Shelter and adoption are the two humane society programs most familiar to the American public. Less known to the public are the numerous other programs and services—all of which help animals in need and keep humane society workers busy around the clock, seven days a week.

Abuse and Neglect Investigation

Across the country, humane society abuse investigators seize thousands of animals every year from abusive conditions. Many are dogs and roosters trained for fighting. Others are victims of cruelty, such as the dog that was left on her chain for days on end, exposed to the cold and having little water to drink. Her owner threw her food just once a week but otherwise ignored her.

The dog tugged on her chain repeatedly, trying to escape these miserable conditions. When a humane society abuse investigator rescued the dog, he discovered her chain had cut deeply into her neck.

Abuse investigators also come to the aid of many animals that are victims of neglect. Some owners neglect their pets out of ignorance. Unaware of their pets' needs, these people don't provide them with adequate shelter, food, or water. Or they leave their animals home alone for too long. Or they don't realize that as puppies and kittens grow, larger collars are needed. Collars that are too tight have choked many puppies and kittens as they grow into adulthood.

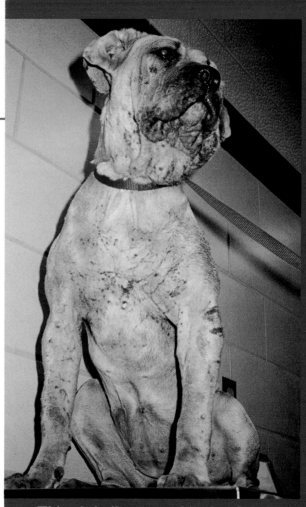

This pit bull was used in dog fighting before it was seized by a humane society abuse investigator.

Every year in America, abuse officers receive thousands of phone calls from concerned citizens who witness animals suffering from abuse and neglect. When an investigator receives a call, he or she visits the home of the troubled pet. The investigator offers humane education to the pet owner, and sometimes that's enough to correct the problem. But if the life or well-being of the animal is at stake, the investigator may seize the pet.

Investigators prosecute people, including minors, for abusing animals. Children who shoot small animals with BB guns— not for food or to hunt during legal hunting seasons, but for malicious entertainment—are committing criminal acts.

Investigators have taken minors to court for such crimes. Often, these children come from abusive homes. Humane societies want judges to put the children into counseling programs so that this type of abuse will end.

Not all humane societies have the funds for abuse and neglect investigation. Smaller or rural communities that lack investigators forward calls to city police agencies and county sheriff departments, which work with state investigators to handle abuse cases.

Humane Education

Only through education can people become aware of and sensitive to the needs of all creatures. Humane societies consider it their duty to teach children and adults about the proper treatment of animals.

It's especially important to introduce humane education to people when they're young. Humane societies believe they can change the way animals are treated tomorrow by helping to educate children today.

Education is central to humane society services. Humane education teaches that all animals—domestic and wild alike— have the right not to be abused. It encourages people to question the idea that animals exist for human benefit. Humane education also helps people to be more sympathetic to animals by emphasizing the many similarities between humans and animals. And it teaches that people don't have to love animals but that they should treat animals with respect and consideration.

Humane society volunteers visit classrooms and Scout troops across America, offering a variety of lessons in humane education. Much of what they teach concerns companion animals. Young children, for instance, learn the proper way to hold a puppy. Humane educators also teach how important it is never to hit a pet in anger or as a matter of discipline. Hitting does not teach a cat or dog right from wrong. An effective way to discipline pets is to praise their desirable behavior.

At some larger shelters, education programs include summer camps, where children learn about farm and wild animals as well as companion animals. Some larger shelters also sponsor pet shows, where children experience pride in taking responsible care of a living creature.

Animal Information Services

"Who can help an injured hawk?" "How do you housebreak a rabbit?" Each day, humane society workers across the country answer thousands of animal-related questions over the telephone. Shelters also offer information to the public through classes, books, bulletins, videos, and pamphlets.

Some large shelters offer summer camps that teach children about all sorts of living creatures, including farm animals.

Most humane society shelters offer in-depth information about the proper care of pets. Much of it concerns proper canine care. One pamphlet instructs owners never to leave their dogs in cars during hot weather—even with the windows open several inches. A car will quickly become hot enough to cause heat stroke in a dog. If the condition goes unchecked, the animal could go into a coma and die. Another pamphlet warns against letting dogs travel unsecured in the back of pickup trucks. Sudden starts, stops, and turns can toss the dogs onto the road. Every year, numerous canines are killed this way. If falling onto the road doesn't kill them, oncoming traffic does.

Humane societies also offer much information about proper cat care. They especially want the public to know this fact about outdoor cats:

CATS + OUTSIDE = AN ACCIDENT WAITING TO HAPPEN

Allowing cats to roam freely, humane society literature tells readers, is risky business. A cat that's kept solely indoors can be expected to live an average of 12 to 15 years or more. But the average life span of an outdoor or indoor-outdoor cat is only 2 to 3 years. Most outdoor cats die from being hit by cars. Others catch rabies from wild animals or are fatally attacked by dogs. Outdoor cats also run the risk of getting lost. Every year, only about five percent of all lost cats are reunited with their owners.

Some people believe it's not natural to keep cats entirely indoors. But domesticated cats aren't wild predators. They're dependent on humans, receiving everything they need from people. In today's world, cats can no longer safely roam outdoors, hunting for their prey.

By providing pet owners with facts such as these, humane society Animal Information Services help save lives. All shelters have some materials available to the public, and they can direct people to other sources for additional information.

Foster Care

Bleary-eyed, a woman gets out of bed at three o'clock in the morning to feed a litter of orphaned kittens. For several weeks, she bottle feeds the tiny babies every four hours around the clock. As the kittens grow older, the woman invites neighborhood children over to play with them. This socializes the kittens, helping them to feel comfortable with children as well as adults. If the kittens like children, they'll be more adoptable.

This woman is a "foster parent" in her area humane society foster care program. Across the country, humane society volunteers take animals into their homes for temporary care before they're adopted. Animals surrendered to shelters often need one-on-one care that's best provided in a private home. This is especially true for pregnant dogs and cats, litters that are still too young for adoption, and sick or injured animals that need rehabilitation. Foster parents also help develop adoptable animals out of unadoptable ones—by encouraging the animals to overcome shyness and fear or by working to housebreak them.

Many shelters also have foster programs for strays. They place the strays with foster families for about a week to find out if the animals are housebroken, if they relate well to children or other animals, and if they know any tricks or commands. This information makes the strays more adoptable. Not all humane society shelters are able to have foster care programs. It depends on the number of volunteers available in each community.

Pet Therapy

One afternoon in a nursing home, a normally unhappy and quiet resident has a four-legged visitor named Homer. The nursing home employees are astounded when they see the resident's eyes sparkle and hear her say, "You're a good dog, Homer." These are the first words the woman has spoken after years of silence.

Across America, humane society volunteers visit lonely and sick people in nursing homes, children's hospitals, and other institutions. But they don't go alone. They take along puppies, kittens, dogs, cats, rabbits, guinea pigs, and other cuddly or friendly shelter animals. The animals spend time with the residents.

Pet therapy is one program offered by humane societies that benefits people.

While most humane society services help needy animals, this program helps needy people. It's called pet therapy. Studies show that human-animal contact has a positive effect on the well-being of recovering patients. Exposure to animals improves people's blood pressure and their respiration and heart rates. It also curbs loneliness. And being with animals helps handicapped and ill people feel accepted as they are—since animals aren't critical and never judge anyone.

Researchers have also discovered these facts about human-animal contact: Disturbed children in institutions become calmer in the presence of animals; people of all ages who have a hard time talking find it easier to start a conversation when pets are nearby; and nursing home residents exposed to pets are more alert. Scientists say it's a proven fact—being around animals makes people feel better, mentally and physically.

It's true that animals are capable of giving tremendous joy to humans. This is clear in pet therapy programs. But humane societies believe all creatures should be cared for in their own right, regardless of what animals offer to people. Through their services such as foster care and abuse and neglect investigation, humane societies stay busy round-the-clock, putting this philosophy into practice.

A World of Animals

Here in the United States, two national humane societies exist to protect animals. And one international humane society offers protection to animals in all areas of the globe. These three organizations are not shelters like local humane societies. Instead, they're large agencies established to help millions of needy animals in a vast variety of ways.

The American Humane Association

Founded in 1877, the American Humane Association (AHA) is the oldest national organization in the United States dedicated to protecting animals. Among the AHA's hundreds of programs and campaigns, the agency works to outlaw puppy mills, to ban cruel steel-jaw leghold traps used in the fur trade, and to make animals in America's national wildlife refuges safe from hunters. The AHA also works with local animal-care and control agencies to provide them with training and educational materials.

The AHA's Emergency Animal Relief program aids animals across the country when natural disasters strike. The AHA immediately reacts to the needs of the animals in the devastated areas by sending volunteers, water, food, equipment, medicines, and other needed supplies. In 1992, AHA volunteers arrived the day after Hurricane Andrew struck Florida and quickly set up emergency clinics to treat dogs, cats, and horses injured in the hurricane. During the 1993 floods in the Midwest, AHA volunteers spent almost eight weeks covering miles along the flooded Mississippi River, distributing 150,000 pounds of pet food, more than 4,000 vaccines, and 2,000 pounds of cat litter.

The AHA's Los Angeles branch has one primary purpose—to protect animals in the entertainment industry. When animals act in movies and television shows, AHA representatives are on the set to make sure animals aren't neglected or abused.

Years ago, before the AHA began supervising film productions, horses had been painfully and frighteningly tripped with wires when scenes required them to fall

The American Humane Association monitors animal treatment during film and television production. Here the AHA is on location for the shooting of *Back to the Future Part III.*

down. This technique is no longer used, thanks to the AHA's guidelines for treatment of animal actors. Today, when horses must fall in movie or television scenes, the AHA requires that the animals be specially trained to perform the stunts safely. The AHA also requires that the horses fall in a 20-square-foot area that is filled with at least 18 inches of sand to soften the landing. AHA representatives step in to protect animals whenever necessary during filmings, such as when a horse is saddled incorrectly or has run too much. As long as the AHA monitors productions, four-legged movie and television stars will have far more pleasant careers.

The Humane Society of the United States

During the 1950s many Americans had become aware of cruelties to animals that existed in some of the nation's research laboratories and slaughterhouses. These concerned Americans joined forces in 1954 and founded the Humane Society of the United States (HSUS). The new agency immediately began vigorous, nationwide campaigns to combat these cruelties.

In the 40 years since its foundation, the HSUS has grown to be the largest humane society in America today. The HSUS's large membership gives it a strong voice that helps bring about change. In 1992, for instance, the commercial dog-breeding industry admitted that puppy sales decreased that year by one third, due to the HSUS's national campaign against puppy mills. This campaign also caused many cruel breeding establishments to close down.

At times, the HSUS must use legal means to work toward change. One famous HSUS court case involved an Asian elephant named Lota. In 1990 after Lota had spent 36 years in the Milwaukee County Zoo, the zoo no longer wanted her and gave her away to a circus. But according to many witnesses, Lota was brutally beaten by the zoo's elephant handlers during the move from the zoo to the circus, in their attempt to get the frightened elephant into the truck. The HSUS investigated and heard more accounts of other elephant "mishandling" at this zoo. The agency looked for a way to help these zoo elephants and to prevent Lota from having to spend the rest of her life as a circus performer.

The HSUS studied every animal-related federal law and in 1991 sued the United States government for breaking the law regarding the Endangered Species Act. This act states that endangered species—such as Lota, an Asian elephant—must not be transferred to profit-making companies, such as a circus. The court turned down the appeal in late 1994, saying that the Endangered Species Act had not been

Lota, the elephant, being moved by handlers at the Milwaukee County Zoo.

violated by transferring Lota to the circus, and she remains there today. But the pressure the HSUS placed on the zoo to change the way it handled elephants resulted in a victory. In 1994 a Milwaukee public official ordered the two remaining Asian elephants—Tamara and Anne—to be sent to an animal sanctuary in California. In the summer of 1995 the animals were transferred to the sanctuary, where they will live the rest of their lives in dignity and peace.

The World Society for the Protection of Animals

Imagine all the major humane societies in the world joining together to form one very large humane society. They've done so, and the organization is known as the World Society for the Protection of Animals (WSPA). For 40 years, this federation, or league, of humane societies has had the most widespread animal protection network on Earth. Today, more than 300 humane societies from 72 countries belong to the WSPA, including the American Humane Association and the Humane Society of the United States.

The WSPA is the glue that keeps all of its member societies working together rather than against each other. At annual meetings they reach agreements on animal protection issues. This united front gives the WSPA a powerful voice and a great deal of international influence. The WSPA applies this strength in programs that require a global approach, such as their no-fur campaign and their Libearty campaign. The Libearty campaign aims to protect bears, which are some of the most persecuted animals on Earth. Five of the eight bear species are close to extinction.

One of Libearty's success stories involves work with "dancing bears." In southern Europe, Turkey, and India, bears have been forced to endure cruel training to learn to dance. The trainers beat them into obedience, force them to dance on burning metal trays, and pierce their noses with steel rings. The trainers pull

Dancing bears are chained by their trainers and made to perform on the streets.

the bears around by these rings, which rip the animals' skin. The bears perform and pose for tourists who pay money to watch the spectacle.

This practice is illegal in Greece, Turkey, and India, but the bear trainers continue it in spite of the laws. Before 1992 the police never rescued any dancing bears because they had nowhere to keep them. That year, the WSPA found a solution—the agency located 25 acres of land in northern Greece and created a dancing bear refuge. In 1993, with the Greek government's approval, the WSPA raided bear trainers' homes in Greece and rescued three dancing bears. The WSPA has rescued more bears since then and has opened a second sanctuary in Turkey. The rescued bears will spend the remainder of their lives in peace and safety at the dancing bear refuge.

Among its hundreds of other programs, the agency conducts disaster relief operations for natural disasters and human-caused disasters, such as wars. In 1991 the WSPA helped bird and marine life during the Persian Gulf War, which resulted in the biggest oil slick in history. The WSPA also responds quickly to the animal victims of floods, earthquakes, fires, and volcanic eruptions. As John Walsh, the WSPA's international projects director, says, "We try to assist any animal anywhere in the world that needs help."

When John Walsh went to war-torn Bosnia in 1992 to help animal victims of the war, some people questioned his efforts. Why, they wondered, was he working to save animals when so many humans were suffering and dying from the war?

Walsh replied, "There are 29 international relief organizations here for people. But there's only one organization in Bosnia for animals—and that's us."

Humane societies believe it's their obligation to help all animals in need—from a frightened cat clinging to a treetop during a flood, to a dolphin caught in a fisherman's drift net, to an unwanted puppy found in a dumpster.

Whether it's at a small Wisconsin shelter or a large agency in Washington, D.C., humane society volunteers and employees work to relieve the suffering of animals. They will continue to help in whatever ways they can and to speak out for those who can't speak for themselves— because millions of animals throughout the world are depending on them.

Glossary

animal control agency A government funded and operated agency that licenses pets, controls strays and problem animals, and enforces animal-related laws

boycott To refuse to do business or have dealings with someone

canine Any animal of the dog family

endangered Threatened or in danger of extinction

euthanize To put to death painlessly

humane Kind, tender, merciful, sympathetic

immunization Medical treatment that protects an individual from disease

inhumane Lacking kindness

malicious Purposefully hurtful to someone or something

neuter To remove the reproductive organs of a male animal to prevent it from breeding

picket To stand or march back and forth in protest of something

puppy mill A breeding farm where dogs are bred to produce large numbers of puppies

rehabilitate To restore to a condition of good health

sanctuary A natural area where wild animals are protected

slaughterhouse A place where animals are butchered for food

spay To remove the reproductive organs of a female animal to prevent it from breeding

therapy The treatment of an illness of the mind or body

For More Information

For more information about humane societies and their programs please write to:

The American Humane Association
   Animal Protection Division
63 Inverness Drive East
Englewood, Colorado 80112

The American Society for the
   Prevention of Cruelty to Animals
424 East 92nd Street
New York, New York 10128

The Humane Society of the United
   States
2100 L Street Northwest
Washington, D.C. 20037

The World Society for the Protection
   of Animals
P.O. Box 190
Boston, MA 02130

To find the addresses and telephone numbers of local humane societies, please ask a librarian or teacher for assistance or check the yellow pages of the telephone book under "Humane Societies" or "Animal Shelters."

Index

About the Author

As a child, Shelley Swanson Sateren owned a duck named Willy, a goat named Heidi, dozens of goldfish and guppies, a cat, two white rats, four dogs, and a rabbit. Her goat and dogs were adopted from humane societies. Today, Sateren owns an eight-year-old West Highland White Terrier named Max, a stray she also adopted from a humane society.

Sateren has worked as a children's book editor and as a clerk in a children's bookstore. She is also a certified elementary school teacher. The author has written stories and articles for magazines and one book for adults. This is her fourth book for children. She lives in St. Paul, Minnesota, with her husband and young son.

Author Shelley Sateren with her dog Max.